CALIFORNIA
NATIVE AMERICAN TRIBES

YUKI TRIBE

by
Mary Null Boulé

Illustrated by
Daniel Liddell

Merryant Publishers, Inc.
Vashon, WA 98070
206-463-3879

Book Number Twenty-five in a series of twenty-eight

This series is dedicated to Virginia Harding, whose editing expertise and friendship brought this project to fruition.

Library of Congress Catalog Card Number: 92-61897

ISBN: 1-877599-47-6

Copyright © 1992, Merryant Publishing

7615 S.W. 257th St., Vashon, WA 98070.

FOREWORD

Native American people of the United States are often living their lives away from major cities and away from what we call the mainstream of life. It is, then, interesting to learn of the important part these remote tribal members play in our everyday lives.

More than 60% of our foods come from the ancient Native American's diet. Farming methods of today also can be traced back to how tribal women grew crops of corn and grain. Many of our present day ideas of democracy have been taken from tribal governments. Even some 1,500 Native American words are found in our English language today.

Fur traders bought furs from tribal hunters for small amounts of money, sold them to Europeans and Asians for a great deal of money, and became rich. Using their money to buy land and to build office buildings, some traders started business corporations which are now the base of our country's economy.

There has never been enough credit given to these early Americans who took such good care of our country when it was still in their care. The time has come to realize tribal contributions to our society today and to give Native Americans not only the credit, but the respect due them.

Mary Boulé

A-frame cradle for girls; tule matting. Tubatulabal tribe.

GENERAL INFORMATION

Out of Asia, many thousands of years ago, came Wanderers. Some historians think they were the first people to set foot on our western hemisphere. These Wanderers had walked, step by step, onto our part of the earth while hunting and gathering food. They probably never even knew they had moved from one continent to another as they made their way across a land bridge, a narrow strip of land between Siberia and what is now Russia, and the state of Alaska.

Historians do not know exactly how long ago the Wanderers might have crossed the land bridge. Some of them say 35,000 years ago. What historians do know is that these people slowly moved down onto land that we now call the United States of America. Today it would be very hard to follow their footsteps, for the land bridge has been covered with sea water since the thawing of the ice age.

Those Wanderers who made their way to California were very lucky, indeed. California was a land with good weather most of the year and was filled with plenty of plant and animal foods for them to eat.

The Wanderers who became California's Native Americans did not organize into large tribes like the rest of the North American tribes. Instead, they divided into groups, or tribelets, sometimes having as many as 250 people. A tribelet could number as few as three, to as many as thirty villages located close to each other. Some tribelets had only one chief, a leader who lived in the largest village. Many tribes had a chief for each village. Some leaders had no real power but were thought to be wise. Tribal members always listened with respect to what their chief had to say.

From 20 to 100 people could be living in one village, which usually had several houses. In most cases, these groups of people were related to each other. From five to ten people of one family lived in one house. For instance, a mother, a

4

father, two or three children, a grandmother, or aunt or daughter-in-law might live together.

Village members together would own the land important to them for their well-being. Their land might include oak trees with precious acorns, streams and rivers, and plants which were good to eat. Streams and rivers were especially important to a tribe's quality of life. Water drew animals to it; that meant more food for the tribe to eat. Fish were a good source of food, and traveling by boat was often easier than walking long distances. Water was needed in every part of tribal life.

Village and tribelet land was carefully guarded. Each group knew exactly where the boundaries of its land were found. Boundaries were known by landmarks such as mountains or rivers, or they might also be marked by poles planted in the ground. Some boundary lines were marked by rocks, or by objects placed there by tribal members. The size of a territory had to be large enough to supply food to every person living there.

The California tribes spoke many languages. Sometimes villages close together even had a problem understanding one another. This meant that each group had to be sure of the boundaries of other tribes around them when gathering food. It would not be wise to go against the boundaries and the customs of neighbors. The Native Americans found if they respected the boundaries of their neighbors, not so many wars had to be fought. California tribes, in spite of all their differences, were not as warlike as other tribes in our country.

Not only did the California tribes speak different languages, but their members also differed in size. Some tribes were very tall, almost six feet tall. The shortest people came from the Yuki tribe which had territory in what is now Mendocino County. They measured only about 5'2" tall. All Native Americans, regardless of size, had strong, straight black hair and dark brown eyes.

TRADE

Trading between tribes was an important part of life. Inland tribes had large animal hides that coastal tribes wanted. By trading the hides to coastal groups, inland tribes would receive fish and shells, which they in turn wanted. Coastal tribes also wanted minerals and rocks mined in the mountains by inland tribes. Obsidian rock from the northern mountains was especially wanted for arrowheads. There were, as well, several minerals, mined in the inland mountains, which could be made into the colorful body paints needed for religious ceremonies.

Southern tribes particularly wanted steatite from the Gabrielino tribe. Steatite, or soapstone, was a special metal which allowed heat to spread evenly through it. This made it a good choice to be used for cooking pots and flat frying pans. It could be carved into bowls because of its softness and could be decorated by carving designs into it. Steatite came from Catalina Island in the Coastal Gabrielino territory. Gabrielinos found steatite to be a fine trading item to offer for the acorns, deerskins, or obsidian stone they needed.

When people had no items to trade but needed something, they used small strings of shells for money. The small dentalium shells, which came from the far distant Northwest coast, had great value. Strings of dentalia usually served as money in the Northern California tribes, although some dentalia was used in the Central California tribes.

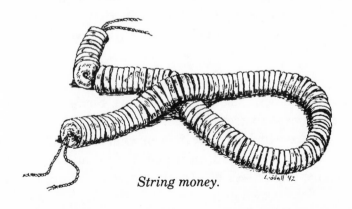

String money.

In southern California clam shells were broken and holes were bored through the center of each piece. Then the pieces were rounded and polished with sandstone and strung into strings for money. These were not thought to be as valuable as dentalia.

Strings of shell money were measured by tattoo marks on the trader's lower arm or hand.

Here is a sample of shell value:

> A house, three strings
> A fishing place, one to three strings
> Land with acorn-bearing oak trees, one to five strings

A great deal of rock and stone was traded among the tribes for making tools. Arrows had to have sharp-edged stone for tips. The best stone for arrow tips was obsidian (volcanic glass) because, when hit properly, it broke off into flakes with very sharp edges. California tribes considered obsidian to be the most valuable rock for trading.

Some tribes had craftsmen who made knives with wooden handles and obsidian blades. Often the handles were decorated with carvings. Such knives were good for trading purposes. Stone mortars and pestles, used by the women for grinding grains into flour, were good trading items.

BASKETS & POTTERY

California tribal women made beautiful baskets. The Pomo and Chumash baskets, what few are left, show us that the women of those tribes might have been some of the finest basketmakers in the world. Baskets were used for gathering and storing food, for carrying babies, and even for hauling water. In emergencies, such as flooding waters, sometimes children, women, and tribal belongings crossed the swollen rivers and streams in huge, woven baskets! Baskets were so tightly woven that not a drop of water could leak from them.

Baskets also made fine cooking pots. Very hot rocks were taken from a fire and tossed around inside baskets with a looped tree branch until food in the basket was cooked.

Most baskets were made to do a certain job, but some baskets were designed for their beauty alone and were excellent for trading. Older women of a tribe would teach young girls how to weave baskets.

Pottery was not used by many California tribes. What little there was seems to have been made by those tribes living near to the Navaho and Mohave tribes of Arizona, and it shows their style. For example, pottery of the California tribes did not have much decoration and was usually a dull red color. Designs were few and always in yellow.

Ohlone hunter wearing deerskin camouflage.

Long thin coils of clay were laid one on top the other. Then the coils were smoothed between a wooden paddle and a small stone to shape the bowl. Pottery from California Native Americans has been described as light weight and brittle (easily broken), probably because of the kind of clay soil found in California.

HUNTING & FISHING

Tribal men spent much of their time making hunting and fishing tools. Bows and arrows were built with great care, to make them shoot as accurately as possible. Carelessly made hunting weapons caused fewer animals to be killed and people then had less food to eat.

Bows made by men of Southern California tribes were made long and narrow. In the northern part of the state bows were a little shorter, thinner, and wider than those of their northern neighbors. Size and thickness of bows depended on the size trees growing in a tribe's territory. The strongest bows were wrapped with sinew, the name given to animal tendons. Sinew is strong and elastic like a rubber band.

Arrows were made in many sizes and shapes, depending on their use. For hunting larger animals, a two-piece arrow was used. The front piece of the arrow shaft was made so that it would remain in the animal, even if the back part was removed or broken off. The arrowhead, or point, was wrapped to the front piece of the shaft. This kind of arrow was also used in wars.

Young boys used a simple wooden arrow with the end sharpened to a point. With this they could hunt small animals like birds and rabbits. The older men of the tribe taught boys how to make their own arrows, how to aim properly, and how to repair broken weapons.

Tribal men spent many hours making and mending fishing nets. The string used in making nets often came from the fibers of plants. These fibers were twisted to make them strong and tough, then knotted into netting. Fences, or weirs, that had one small opening for fish, were built across streams. As the fish swam through the opening they would be caught in netting or harpooned by a waiting fisherman.

Hooks, if used at all, were cut from shells. Mostly hooks could be found when the men fished in large lakes or when catching trout in high mountain areas. Hooks were attached to heavy plant fiber string.

Dip nets, made of netting attached to branches that were bent into a circle, were used to catch fish swimming near shore. Dip nets had long handles so the fishermen could reach deep into the water.

Sometimes a mild poison was placed on the surface of shallow water. This confused the fish and caused them to float to the surface of the water, where they could be scooped up by a waiting fisherman. Not enough poison was used to make humans ill.

Not all fishing was done from the shore. California tribes used two kinds of boats when fishing. Canoes, dug out of one half a log, were useful for river fishing. These were square at each end, round on the bottom, and very heavy. Some of them were well-finished, often even having a carved seat in them.

Today we think of "balsa" as a very lightweight wood, but in Spanish, the word balsa means "raft". That is why Spanish explorers called the Native American canoes, made from tule reeds, "balsa" boats.

Balsa boats were made of bundled tule reeds and were used throughout most of California. They made into safe, light-weight boats for lake and river use. Usually the balsa canoe had a long, tightly tied bundle of tule for the boat bottom and one bundle for each side of the canoe. The front of the canoe was higher than the back. Balsa boats could be steered with a pole or with a paddle, like a raft.

Men did most of the fishing, women were in charge of gathering grasses, seeds, and acorns for food. After the food was collected, it was either eaten right away or made ready for winter storage.

Except for a few southern groups, California tribes had perma-nent villages where they lived most of the year. They also had food-gathering places they returned to each year to collect acorns, salt, fish, and other foods not found near their villages.

FOOD

Many different kinds of plant food grew wild in California in the days before white people arrived. Berries and other plant foods grew in the mountains. Forests offered the local tribes everything from pine nuts to animals.

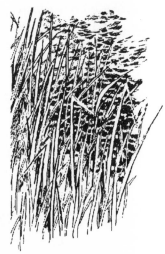

Native Americans found streams full of fish for much of the year. Inland fresh water lakes had large tule reeds growing along their shores. Tule could be eaten as food when plants were young and tender. More important, however, tule was used in making fabric for clothes and for building boats and houses. Tule was probably the most useful plant the California Native Americans found growing wild in their land.

Like all deserts, the one in southern California had little water or fish, but small animals and cactus plants made good food for the local tribes. They moved from place to place harvesting whatever was ripe. Tribal members always knew when and where to find the best food in their territory.

Acorns were the main source of food for all California tribes. Acorn flour was as important to the California Native Americans as wheat is to us today. Five types of California oak trees produced acorns that could be eaten. Those from black oak and tanbark oak seem to have been the favorite kinds.

Since some acorns tasted better than others, the tastiest ones were collected first. If harvest of the favorite acorn was poor some years, then less tasty acorns had to be eaten all winter long.

So important were acorns to California Indians that most tribes built their entire year around them. Acorn harvest marked the beginning of their calendar year. Winter was counted as so many months after acorn harvest, and summer was counted by the number of months before the next acorn harvest.

Acorn harvest ceremonies usually were the biggest events of the year. Most celebrations took place in mid-October and included dancing, feasts, games of chance, and reunions with relatives. Harvest festivals lasted for many days. They were a time of joy for everyone.

The annual acorn gathering lasted two to three weeks. Young boys climbed the oak trees to shake branches; some men used long poles to knock acorns to the ground. Women loaded the nuts into large cone-shaped burden baskets and carried them to a central place where they were put in the sun to dry.

Once the acorns were dried, the women carried them back to the tribe's permanent villages. There they lined special basket-like storage granaries with strong herbs to keep insects away, then stored the acorns inside. Granaries were placed on stilts to keep animals from getting into them and were kept beside tribal houses.

Preparing acorns for each meal was also the women's job. Shells were peeled by hitting the acorns with a stone hammer on an anvil (flat) stone. Meat from the nut was then laid on a stone mortar. A mortar was usually a large stone with a slight dip on its surface. Sometimes the mortar had a bottomless basket, called a hopper, glued to its top. This kept the acorn meat from sliding off the mortar as it was beaten. The meat was then pounded with a long stone pestle. Acorn flour was scraped away from the hopper's sides with a soaproot fiber brush during this process.

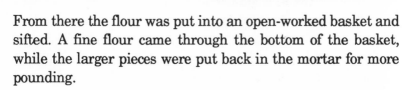

From there the flour was put into an open-worked basket and sifted. A fine flour came through the bottom of the basket, while the larger pieces were put back in the mortar for more pounding.

The most important process came after the acorn flour was sifted. Acorn flour has a very bitter-tasting tannin in it. This bitter taste was removed by a method called leaching. Many tribes leached the flour by first scooping out a hollow in sand near water. The hollow was lined with leaves to keep the flour from washing away. A great deal of hot water was poured through the flour to wash out (leach) the bitterness. Sometimes the flour was put into a basket for the leaching process, instead of using sand and leaves.

Finally the acorn flour was ready to be cooked. To make mush, heated stones were placed in the basket with the flour. A looped tree branch or two long sticks were used to toss the hot rocks around so the basket would not burn. When the mush had boiled, it could be eaten. If the flour and water mixture was baked in an earthen oven, it became a kind of bread. Early explorers wrote that it was very tasty.

Historians have estimated that one family would eat from 1500 to 2000 pounds of acorn flour a year. One reason California native Americans did not have to plant seeds and raise crops was because there were so many acorns for them to harvest each year.

Whether they ate fish or shellfish or plant food or animal meat, nature supplied more than enough food for the Native Americans who lived in California long ago. Many believed their good fortune in having fine weather and plenty to eat came from being good to their gods.

RELIGION

Tribal members had strong beliefs in the power of spirits or gods around them. Each tribe was different, but all felt the importance of never making a spirit angry with them. For that reason a celebration to thank the spirit-gods for treating them well, took place before each food gathering and before each hunting trip, and after each food harvest.

Usually spiritual powers were thought to belong to birds or animals. Most California tribespeople felt bears were very wicked and should not be eaten. But Coyote seems to have been a kind leader who helped them if they were in trouble, even though he seems to have been a bit naughty at times. Eagle was thought to be very powerful and good to native Americans. In some tribes, Eagle was almost as powerful as Sun.

Tribes placed importance on different gods, according to the tribe's needs. Rain gods were the most important spirits to desert tribes. Weather gods, who might bring less rain or warmer temperatures, were important to northern tribes. A great many groups felt there were gods for each of the winds: North, South, East and West. The four directions were usually included in their ceremonial dances and were used as part of the decorations on baskets, pots, and even tools.

Animals were not only worshipped and believed to be spirit-gods, like Deer or Antelope, but tribal members felt there was a personal animal guardian for each one of them. If a tribal member had a deer as guardian, then that person could never kill a deer or eat deer meat.

California Native Americans believed in life after death. This made them very respectful of death and very fearful of angering a dead person. Once someone died, the name of the dead person could never again be said aloud. Since it was easy to accidentally say a name aloud, the name was usually given to a new baby. Then the dead person would not become angry.

Shamans were thought to be the keepers of religious beliefs and to have the ability to talk directly to spirit-gods. It was the job of a village shaman to cure sick people, and to speak to the gods about the needs of the people. Some tribes had several kinds of shamans in one village. One shaman did curing, one scared off evil spirits, while another took care of hunters.

Not all shamans were nice, so people greatly feared their power. However, if shamans had no luck curing sick people or did not bring good luck in hunting, the people could kill them. Most shamans were men, but in a few tribes, women were doctors.

Most California tribal myths have been lost to history because they were spoken and never written down. The legends were told and retold on winter nights around the home fires. Sadly, these were forgotten after the missionaries brought Christianity to California and moved tribal members into the missions.

A few stories still remain, however. It is thought by historians that northwest California tribes were the only ones not to have a myth on how they were created. They did not feel that the world was made and prepared for human beings. Instead, their few remaining stories usually tell of mountain peaks or rivers in their own territory.

The central California tribes had creation stories of a great flood where there was only water on earth. They tell of how man was made from a bit of mud that a turtle brought up from the bottom of the water.

Many southwest tribes believed there was a time of no sky or water. They told of two clouds appearing which finally became Sky and Earth.

Throughout California, however, all tribes had myths that told of Eagle as the leader, Coyote as chief assistant, and of less powerful spirits like Falcon or Hawk.

Costumes for religious ceremonies often imitated these animals they worshipped or feared. Much time was spent in making the dance costumes as beautiful as possible. Red woodpecker feathers were so brilliant a color they were used to decorate religious headdresses, necklaces, or belts. Deerskin clothing was fringed so shell beads could be attached to each thin strip of leather.

Eagle feathers were felt to be the most sacred of religious objects. Sometimes they were made into whole robes.

Religious feather charm.

Usually, though, the feathers were used just for decorations. All these costumes were valuable to the people of each tribe. The village chief was in charge of taking care of the costumes, and there was terrible punishment for stealing them. Clothing worn everyday was not fancy like costuming for rituals.

Willow bark skirt.

CLOTHING

Central and southern California's fine weather made regular clothes not really very important to the Native Americans. The children and men went naked most of the year, but most women wore a short apron-like skirt. These skirts were usually made in two pieces, front and back aprons, with fringes cut into the bottom edges. Often the skirt was made from the inner bark of trees, shredded and gathered on a cord. Sometimes the skirt was made from tule or grass.

In northern California and in rainy or windy weather elsewhere in the state, animal-skin blankets were worn by both men and women. They were used like a cape and wrapped around the body. Sometimes the cape was put over one shoulder and under the other arm, then tied in front. All kinds of skins were used; deer, otter, wildcat, but sea-otter fur was thought to be the best. If the skin was from a small animal, it was cut into strips and woven together into a fabric. At night the cape became a blanket to keep the person warm.

Because of the rainy weather in northern California, the women wore basket caps all the time. Women of the central and south tribes wore caps only when carrying heavy loads, where the forehead had to be used as support. Then a cap helped keep too much weight from being placed on the forehead.

Most California people went barefoot in their villages. For journeys into rough land, going to war, wood gathering, or in colder weather, the tribesmen in central and northwest California wore a one-piece soft shoe with no extra sole, which went high up on the leg.

Southern California tribespeople, however, wore sandals most of the time, wearing high, soled moccasins only when they traveled long distances or into the mountains. Leggings of skin were worn in snow, and moccasins were sometimes lined with grass for more comfort and warmth.

VILLAGE LIFE

Houses of the California tribes were made of materials found in their area. Usually they were round with domed roofs. Except for a few tribes, a house floor was dug into the earth a few feet. This was wise, for it made the home warmer in winter and cooler in summer. It also meant that less material was needed to make house walls.

Framework for the walls was made from bendable branches tied to support poles. Some frames of the houses were covered with earth and grass. Others were covered with large slabs of redwood or pine bark. Central California

Split-stick clapper, rhythm instrument. Hupa tribe.

villagers made large woven mats of tule reed to cover the tops and sides of houses. In the warmer southern area, brush and smaller pieces of bark were used for house walls.

Most California Native American villages had a building called a sweathouse, where the men could be found when they were not hunting, fishing or traveling. It was a very important place for the men, who used it rather like a clubhouse. They could sweat and then scrape themselves clean with curved ribs of deer. The sweathouse was smaller than a family house. Normally it had a center pole framework with a firepit on the ground next to the pole. When the fire was lit, some smoke was allowed to escape through a hole at the top of the roof; however, most was trapped inside the building. Smoke and heat were the main reasons for having a sweathouse. Both were believed to be a way to purify tribal members' bodies. Sweathouse walls were mainly hard-packed earth. The heat produced was not a steam heat but came from a wood-fed fire.

In the center of most villages was a large house that often had no walls, just a roof held up with poles. It was here that religious dances and rituals were held, or visitors were entertained.

Dances were enjoyed and were performed with great skill. Music, usually only rhythm instruments, accompanied the dances. For some reason California Native Americans did not use drums to create rhythms for their dances. Three different kinds of rattles were used by California tribes.

One type, split-clap sticks, created rhythm for dancing. These were usually a length of cane (a hollow stick) split in half lengthwise for about two-thirds of its length. The part still uncut was tightly wound with cord so it would not split all the way. The stick was held at the tied end in one hand and hit against the palm of the other hand to make its sound.

A pebble-filled moth cocoon made rhythm for shaman duties. These could range from calling on spirits to cure illnesses, to performing dances to bring rain. Probably the best sounds to beat rhythm for songs and dances came from bundles of deer hooves tied together on a stick. These rattles have a hollow, warm sound.

The only really "musical" instrument found in California was a flute made of reed that was played by blowing across the edge of one end. Melodies were not played on any of these instruments. Most North American Indians sang their songs rather than playing melodies on music instruments.

Special songs were sung for each event. There were songs for healing sick people, songs for success in hunting, war, or marriage. Women sang acorn-grinding songs and lullabies. Songs were sung in sorrow for the dead and during story-telling times. Group singing, with a leader, was the favorite kind of singing. Most songs were sung by all tribe members, but religious songs had to be sung by a special group. It was important that sacred songs not be changed through the years. If a mistake was made while singing sacred music, the singer could be punished, so only specially trained singers would sing ritual songs.

All songs were very short, some of them only 20 to 30 seconds long. They were made longer by repeating the melodies over and over, or by connecting several songs together. Songs usually told no story, just repeated words or phrases or syllables in patterns.

Song melodies used only one or two notes and harmony was never added. Perhaps that is why mission Indians, at those missions with musician priests, especially loved to sing harmony in the church choirs.

Songs and dances were good methods of passing rich tribal traditions on to the children. It was important to tribal adults that their children understand and love the tribe's heritage.

Children were truly wanted by parents in most tribes and new parents carefully watched their tiny babies day and night, to be sure they stayed warm and dry. Usually a newborn was strapped into a cradle and tied to the mother's back so she could continue to work, yet be near the baby at all times. In some tribes, older children took care of babies of cradle age during the day to give the mother time to do all her work, while grandmothers were often in charge of caring for toddlers.

Children were taught good behavior, traditions, and tribal rules from babyhood, although some tribes were stricter than others. Most of the time parents made their children obey. Young children could be lightly punished, but in many tribes those over six or seven years old were more severely punished if they did not follow the rules.

Just as children do today, Native American youngsters had childhood traditions they followed. For instance, one tribal tradition said that when a baby tooth came out, a child waited until dusk, faced the setting sun and threw the tooth to the west. There is no mention of a generous tooth fairy, however.

Tribal parents were worried that their offspring might not be strong and brave. Some tribes felt one way to make their children stronger was by forcing them to bathe in ice cold water, even in wintertime. Every once in a while, for example, Modoc children were awakened from sleep and taken to a cold lake or stream for a freezing bath.

But if freezing baths at night were hard on young Native Americans, their days were carefree and happy. Children were allowed to play all day, and some tribes felt children did not even have to come to dinner if they didn't want to. In those tribes, children could come to their houses to eat anytime of the day.

The games boys played are not too different from those played today. Swimming, hide and seek among the tule reeds, a form of tetherball with a mud ball tied to a pole, and willow-javelin throwing kept boys busy throughout the day.

Fathers made their sons small bows and arrows, so boys spent much time trying to improve their hunting skills. They practised shooting at frogs or chipmunks. The first animal any boy killed was not touched or eaten by him. Others would carry the kill home to be cooked and eaten by villagers. This tradition taught boys always to share food.

Another hunting tool for boys was a hollowed-out willow branch. This became like a modern day beanshooter, only the Native American boys shot juniper berries instead of beans. Slingshots made good hunting weapons, as well.

Girls and boys shared many games, but girls playing with each other had contests to see who could make a basket the fastest, or they played with dolls made of tule. Together, young boys and girls played a type of ring-around-the-rosie game, climbed mountains, or built mud houses.

As children grew older, the boys followed their fathers and the girls followed their mothers as the adults did their daily work. Children were not trained in the arts of hunting or basketmaking, however, until they became teenagers.

HISTORY

Spanish missionaries, led by Fray Junipero Serra, arrived in California in 1769 to build missions along the coast of California. By 1823, fifty years later, 21 missions had been founded. Almost all of them were very successful, and the Franciscan monks who ran them were proud of how many Native Americans became Christians.

However, all was not as the monks had planned it would be. Native American people had never been around the diseases European white men brought with them. As a result, they had no immunity to such illnesses as measles, small pox, or flu. Too many mission Indians died from white men's diseases.

Historians figure there were 300,000 Native Americans living in California before the missionaries came. The missions show records of 83,000 mission Indians during mission days. By the time the Mexicans took over the missions from the Spanish in 1834, only 20,000 remained alive.

The great California Gold Rush of 1849 was probably another big reason why many of the Native Americans died during that time. White men, staking their claim to tribal lands with gold upon it, thought nothing of killing any California tribesman who tried to keep and protect his territory. Fifty-thousand tribal members died from diseases, bullets, or starvation between the gold Rush Days and 1870. By 1910, only 17,000 California Indians remained.

Although the American government tried to set aside reservations (areas reserved for Native Americans), the land given to the Indians often was not good land. Worse yet, some of the land sacred to tribes, such as burial grounds, was taken over by white people and never given back.

Sadly, mission Indians, when they became Christians, forgot the proud heritage and beliefs they had followed for thousands of years. Many wonderful myths and songs they had passed from one generation to the next, on winter nights so long ago, have been lost forever.

Today some 100,000 people can claim California Native American ancestors, but few pure-blooded tribespeople remain. Our link with the Wanderers, who came from Asia so long ago, has been forever broken.

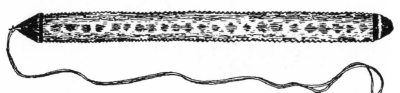

The bullroarer made a deep, loud sound when whirled above the player's head. Tipai tribe.

Villages were usually built beside a lake, stream, or river. Balsa canoes are on the shore. Tule reeds grow along the edge of the water and are drying on poles on the right side of the picture.

24

Women preparing food in baskets, sit on tule mats. Tule mats are being tied to the willow pole framework of a house being built by one of the men.

YUKI TRIBE

INTRODUCTION

There were two main groups of Yuki (You' key) people. The inland tribelet, living in the rugged coastal mountain range along streams of the Eel River, and the coastal tribelet, living in a 50 mile strip along the ocean shoreline of the Mendicino area.

Other than finding evidence that there were possibly 11 group settlements before white people arrived, not much is known of the coastal tribelets. They were called the 'shellmound dwellers' because of the mounds of empty mussel and clam shells they left on the ocean shore as they removed meat from the shells for food.

The inland Yuki people lived in Round Valley. This was the site of an ancient lake, long since dried up. Though given the name Round, it was really oval in shape, seven-and-one-half miles long and five miles wide.

One hundred years ago there were several small streams running through Round Valley that flowed into the Eel River. The land had many fine trees, such as giant oaks, willow, and cottonwood. The valley floor was covered timothy, clover, and many other kinds of grasses and plants. An early settler in 1856 described some grass as so tall it was coming "up even with our horses' backs."

Yuki tribal land on the coast gave way to mountains and forests. Its exact boundaries are not known. However, archeologists who dig for tools and other ancient peoples' belongings, have been busy in this territory for many years.

They have recorded findings of ancient life in nearly 500 places throughout the Yukis' small territory; 255 of those sites are in Round Valley alone. That many sites (locations), and the findings there, indicate to archeologists that large numbers of people lived in tiny Round Valley many hundreds of years before white people came into the area.

Although historians cannot agree on exactly how many Yukis there were in ancient times, one good estimate is 6,880 people, with some 1500 living in Round Valley.

The members of this tribe were the shortest of all the United States Native Americans. Yuki men were only five-feet-2 inches high, (the women were even smaller), and they had broad, straight noses and were deep chested.

In spite of their small size, they were known to be fierce and warlike, and neighboring tribes were quite fearful of them. They were very proud of their fierce reputation.

The mountains of this area were more like foothills, with no more than three feet of snow in wintertime. Summer temperatures went as high as 110°.

Since the climate was warm most of the year, plants and trees thrived in Yuki territory. With plenty of food available all year long, life was fairly easy for the Yuki tribe.

THE VILLAGES

A permanent village was made up of several clusters of homes, rather like suburbs are clustered around a main city today. There were anywhere from one to 25 dwelling houses in a village, and upwards of 150 villagers who lived in these permanent villages during the cold winter months.

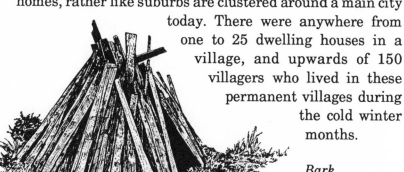

Bark dwelling house.

Villages had names which described where the settlement was built. For instance, one village had the Indian name of *cochohanùk,* meaning 'little oak under water.'

Usually Yuki villages were built in the lower elevations, in valleys, along the edges of streams, and among oak trees. Not many villages were built in the evergreen forests which were mostly found in the high, mountainous parts of the territory. The forests were colder and not as many animals that provided for the tribe lived in forest areas.

Each large village had many multi-family (more than one family) dwelling houses and dance houses. Homes in permanent settlements like these were built of sturdy material to keep out the cold. Tree bark slab walls were laid over a framework made of poles.

The cone-shaped houses for one family were built over a foundation hole which had been dug into the ground one or two feet. The dwelling measured ten feet across at the widest part of the floor.

Dirt which had been dug out to form the round foundation hole was tightly packed between the walls and the ground to keep out winter winds.

Inside, in the center of the dwelling house, was a hollowed out place in the floor for a fire pit that provided heat and a place to cook meals. Belongings such as storage baskets, tools, and bedding were stored on the dirt ledge at the top of the foundation hole. Clothes were hung on the framework poles.

Every village had a dance house which was used for ceremonial rituals, dancing, and entertaining visitors. It was built in the same style as dwelling houses but was much larger, and foundation holes were dug from four to five feet into the earth.

A round dance house might measure 30 to 40 feet in diameter at floor level. Its fir roof beams were covered with earth, and the whole building was supported by one large center pole. Sometimes, the dance house served as a meeting room or a sweathouse.

Many times the sweathouse was a separate building. There, huge fires were built in the fire pit to make the temperature inside hot enough to cause tribal men to sweat. Sweating was believed to purify tribal members' bodies, making them more ready for a hunting or fishing trip.

VILLAGE LIFE

Yuki life centered around the village. Most villagers were related to all tribal members living there. Cousins were considered brothers and sisters.

A leader, or chief, was in charge of village daily life. It was his job to see that his people led a good life. He settled all fights and quarrels among his people. The importance of a person could be shown by where his house was placed in his settlement. If a villager's house was in the center of all home clusters and near the dance-meeting house, he was a powerful tribal leader, indeed.

Earthen round house used for meetings and sweating.

The land, and what grew on it, was owned by all villagers. Women usually owned their own household tools, baskets, and utensils. Men owned their own fishing, hunting, and ceremonial items. Villagers also owned the land upon which their family dwellings were built.

Marriage of a couple was not so much a ceremony as an exchange of gifts between families of the two young people. Unlike many tribes, there was no hard and fast rule about where the newlyweds could live. Yukis did not follow one tribal rule honored by most California tribes: Yuki couples were allowed to speak directly to their in-laws from the beginning of their marriage.

A village baby was born in a special hut, with a trained village woman to take charge of the birth. A relative or friend named the child at birth. The name was not a symbol of anything in particular, and although many other tribes were careful to keep a child's real name a secret, the Yukis were called by their real names, not nicknames.

New Yuki mothers and fathers always followed certain tribal laws about what foods they were allowed to eat. There were also hunting and fishing taboos a father obeyed right after the birth of his child. New parents believed that the obeying of tribal rules and taboos would bring their baby a good, healthy life.

Young children had plenty of time to play while growing up. Many of their games were like those children play today: hide-and-seek, running contests, and games played with dolls, or small bow and arrow sets.

Time was given to teaching children tribal rules and to telling them ancient tribal stories. Girls learned adult chores by watching their mothers gather and prepare foods, while boys learned how to hunt and fish from watching their fathers and elder men of their village.

Although this tribe did not have a teenage ceremony for boys, there was a ceremony when girls became teenagers. The main reason for a girl's ritual ceremony was to make sure she had good fortune in her life. The ceremony also explained to girls how they could help their village as they grew older, by preparing food well and having healthy children.

When they became adults, the young men and women were responsible for all food-gathering and hunting. Older men and women were in charge of training the children and did jobs which took a great deal of time. The older women made baskets and taught younger girls how to weave. Older men made and repaired fish nets and hunting tools.

When Yuki villagers died, they were buried in a bent position, with the knees tucked under their chins, and their bodies were wrapped in an animal skin. The body had to face east when placed in the grave. All of a dead person's belongings were either buried with the body or burned.

A mourning period for the dead lasted for one year. During that time, the closest relatives kept their hair cut short and smeared pitch over their heads and faces. No one was allowed to say the name of a dead person aloud, unless it was given to a newborn child.

WAR AND TRADE

The fierce nature of this tribe meant it was often involved in wars. Many battles were fought because someone from another village or tribe trespassed on Yuki territory. Some battles were arranged, with both sides knowing the time and place of the event. Other wars were more cruel, such as suprise attacks on enemy villages where women and children might be hurt.

Before going to battle, a war dance was celebrated. If the battle was won by a Yuki tribelet, a victory scalp dance was held afterwards. Yuki tribelets fought most often with the Pomo and Nomlaki tribes.

In spite of frequent battles with Pomo tribelets, that tribe and the Huchnom tribelet were the Yukis' main trading partners. Inland Yuki traders offered food products from their territory in exchange for seafood and clamshell beads from coastal tribelets, dentalia shells for money strings, and magnesite, which came from the Pomoan tribes.

Magnesite was a very pretty stone which baked into a reddish color and was then highly polished. It was considered quite valuable by the Yuki people.

RELIGION

There was so much food to be found in Yuki territory, that not as much time was needed to travel to food-gathering campsites as other tribes around them. As a result, the Yukis had more time to organize and perform ceremonies and rituals, which they enjoyed.

Most of these events celebrated their good fortune in having enough food. There were acorn harvest ceremonies and First-Fish rituals, as well as social dances and feasts put on throughout the year. An Acorn Sing was held in January and again in March to thank the creator for sending them many acorns and other foods.

Not only were religious dances and rituals presented at most ceremonies, but contests of strength and games of chance were held at these events, too.

Dancers danced to rhythm instruments and to songs sung by trained singers. A log drum, split-stick rattles, bone and hollow-cane whistles, along with cocoon rattles kept the beat of a dance. Bright costumes of feathered headdresses, beaded dance skirts, and body paints all made religious ceremonies colorful.

Yuki myths told of their beliefs in the creation of the earth. Storytellers told of their supreme being and creator, a god called *Taikomol*, which means 'he who walks alone.' The tribe also believed that besides *Taikomol*, there were many lesser spirits living in the mountains and streams around them.

Tribal myths told of a 'heaven' where dead people, who had been good on earth, went when they died. This myth, and others, were taught to the young men by older village men. During the long winter days spent in a village dance house, they also trained some young men to become shamans.

A second important dance was called the Ghost Dance. During this ceremony, boys were taught about different poisons, and some of the youngsters were also trained to become special shamans who used poison.

There were several kinds of shamans, or doctors. True shamans were those who had become doctors because of a dreamlike encounter with a supernatural spirit. They treated illness by singing and dancing. These shamans became quite specialized, with some only treating rattlesnake bites, others treating broken bones, or infections.

Another kind of non-shaman doctor, always a man, was more like a magician who used sleight-of-hand tricks to cure a patient of pain. This kind of shaman had no supernatural experience before training to become a curing doctor. He trained with older doctors in the Ghost Dance ceremony.

A third kind of shaman was the bear shaman. These kinds of doctors were greatly feared, for they were dangerous. They pretended to transform themselves into real bears.

Double-reed whistle, bound together with sinew, and ends sealed with tar.

©92 Liddell

They were known to kill people. Bear shamans wore bear-skin costumes for their rituals and dances.

FOOD

Animal and plant life was plentiful in Yuki territory, so there was no need to grow their own food. The tribe's main foods were deer, salmon, and acorns. Men did most of the hunting and fishing and women gathered plant foods.

By moving to different parts of their territory during the year, villagers harvested every kind of food they needed, storing what they did not eat fresh. Mussels were collected on the coast certain times of the year. Each autumn, whole families worked together to harvest acorns from oak trees growing in Round Valley.

Clover was gathered in the spring and eaten fresh or steamed. Pinole, made from several kinds of crushed seeds, was a favorite food of the tribe. For pinole the seeds were parched (see glossary), then ground into a flour which was eaten dry by picking it up with the fingertips.

Although the tribe ate clover, seeds, nuts, berries, roots, mushrooms, and other foods, acorns were the most important plant food. Hundreds of pounds of acorns were collected each fall by a family, enough to last through the winter. Shells were cracked, the acorn nutmeat inside dried, then put in large burden baskets to be carried back to the winter village for storage.

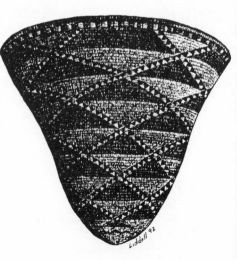

Burden basket.

Acorns were ground into flour every day with mortars and pestles, then cooked and eaten as mush or bread. Acorn flour was used much as we use wheat flour today.

Mortar and pestle with basketry hopper.

During times of salmon runs, when salmon came up the Eel River to lay their eggs, a whole village would move to the river banks while catching fish. Spears, nets, basket traps, weirs, and sometimes mild poison were all used to catch fish.

Usually a weir was built across a smaller stream. It was a dam of brush or rocks with one opening. Sometimes a basket trap was placed at the opening; other times a fisherman might wait at the opening to catch fish in his hands as they came through.

Poison was used to catch fish in the quieter, deeper pools of a river or stream. The mildest poison used was soaproot. The root was pounded into pulp and thrown into the water. Fish were stunned just enough by the poison to float to the surface of the water, where waiting fishermen could pick them up. Fortunately, the poison did not hurt humans.

Yuki hunters believed that each animal killed for food or clothing would be replaced by another. They did not waste any part of animals they did kill. Besides the food and clothing animals provided, their bones were used for tools, eating utensils, sewing needles, musical instruments, or ornaments. Animal tendons were stretchy and so were used to strengthen wood for hunting bows.

Deer were hunted with bows and arrows or caught and held in snares, until they could be killed. Single hunters often

Deerhunter with deerhead disguise.

wore deerheads on their own heads while stalking deer. Tribal hunters were so good at imitating the moves of these animals that they could actually move among a herd of deer, picking which deer they wanted to kill, and never even be noticed by the animals around them.

Yuki hunters only killed bears when necessary, for clothing or food. They never killed grizzly bears, because grizzlies ate humans and Yukis felt this made the bears half-human.

Snares, traps, slings, and bows and arrows were used to kill smaller animals like squirrels, rabbits, or wood rats. Coyotes, otters, foxes, wolves, and panthers were killed for their fur, bones, and tendons, but were never eaten. Beavers and dogs were never killed.

Birds were a good food source for the tribe. Quails were important enough to be killed with special arrows that knocked the birds out rather than killing them.

One favorite food treat was army worms. They appeared on ash trees only every three or four years. Yuki people felt these delicious worms were a gift from their creator, so there was always a special ritual ceremony connected to the harvest of them.

A clap of thunder always seemed to come just before the worms appeared. After the clap of thunder, the entire village would rush to ash trees with baskets of water. Singing, 'Pu, pu, pu,' the villagers held their baskets under the leaves of the trees, and the worms, so the story says, crawled down the tree trunks into the waiting baskets where they drowned in the water. Women then baked the worms, and they were eaten amid celebration and songs.

TOOLS, UTENSILS, AND WEAPONS.

Plants were also sources for other village needs. Cord and string came from fibers of the hemp plant, pine pitch made excellent chewing gum, and mistletoe was important as a medicine.

Wood was used for many of the tribe's needs. Wild mahogany, dogwood, and yew were used to make hunting bows. Arrows were made from the straightest new shoots of elderberry or dogwood.

A

Obsidian arrow point is attached to the front shaft, which sets into the larger back shaft at A. Fletching at the back end of the shaft is of clipped feathers.

© Liddell 92

Larger pieces of wood were made into mortars and pestles for grinding softer foods and medicines. Bark slabs and sturdy tree poles were needed for house building.

Stones were used as hammers, fishnet weights, mortars, and pestles. Obsidian stone (volcanic glass) could be shaped into sharp-edged knife blades, arrow and spear points, and animal hide scrapers. Small stones were used as weapons when shot from a sling.

BASKETS

A beautiful coiled basket.

Yuki women made both twined and coiled baskets. The twined weave was looser and was used for making basket sieves, grain sifters, trays, large burden baskets, seed beaters for collecting seeds, cradles, and hoppers. Basket hoppers were bottomless baskets glued onto stone mortars to keep bits of mashed food from flying off the mortar as it was being ground into flour.

Boiling baskets, and other baskets which needed to be tightly woven, were made using the coiled style of weaving. These baskets were so tightly woven they could even hold water. Food was stored in coiled baskets, as well.

Food was boiled or cooked in baskets by placing very hot stones into the food mixture and tossing the stones with branch loops or two sticks to keep the basket from burning.

Twined baskets were easier to make and were the most used for everyday needs. Coiled baskets were often made to be used as gifts or for trading. This kind of basket was usually decorated with a woven design or pattern.

CLOTHING

Most of the year, men wore only a deerskin cover around their hips, or nothing at all. Children also went without clothes. Women wore fringed deerskin aprons, the larger apron in back and a narrower one in front.

In cooler weather, everyone wore deerskin capes. There is no information on what kind of footwear was worn in the winter. Both men and women wore tattoos and earrings, and sometimes a small bone was put into a pierced nose.

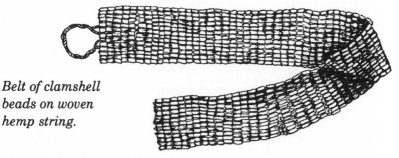

Belt of clamshell beads on woven hemp string.

HISTORY

Yuki tribal members did not have to deal with white people until almost 100 years after the southern and coastal California tribes became a part of the Spanish missions.

In 1856, Round Valley was chosen by the United States government as a reservation for Native Americans. It was one of the first Indian reservations in California. Native Americans from nine different California tribes were placed there. Tribal customs and rituals had to be adjusted to fit many tribes.

Thirty years later, the government gave individual farm plots to some Yuki tribal members. In 1934, the many tribes organized to form a tribal council which still speaks for the needs and wants of those living in Round Valley today.

Although the present-day tribal members still hunt for and gather some of their food, they farm in the manner of their white neighbors. Tribal languages have all but disappeared, but there is new interest in some of the tribes to revive their speaking languages.

While the entire Round Valley was first given to the tribes as a reservation, through the years different pieces of the valley, and its surrounding forest lands, have been given to white settlers.

Today the reservation is made up of many small bits and pieces of land, making it hard for the Native Americans living there to use their land to the fullest. Logging small areas of forest land is far more expensive than logging one large area, and timber is an important industry to tribal members. The Covelo Indian Community Council, in the town of Covelo, is now actively working to make the reservation, once again, a single piece of land.

An estimated 15,000 people of Native American heritage still live in the Round Valley area today, but the last full-blooded Yuki, Rachel Logan, is in her nineties. Recently, she suffered a stroke and can no longer gather grass and seed, as she has done every day of her life. Those who know Mrs. Logan miss seeing her each day, very early in the morning, as she gathered her food for the coming day. It is, sadly, the end of an era in tribal history.

Woman grinding acorns.

YUKI TRIBE
OUTLINE

I. Introduction
- A. Main groups of Yuki people
- B. Round Valley
- C. Description of land
- D. Boundaries of Yuki territory
- E. Archeologists' findings
- F. Description of people
- G. Climate

II. The villages
- A. Description of settlements
- B. Meaning of village names
- C. Location of villages
- D. House descriptions
- E. Dance house description
- F. Sweathouse description

III. Village life
- A. Leader or chief
  - 1. Duties
- B. Land ownership
- C. Marriage
- D. Childbirth
  - 1. Rituals
  - 2. Naming of child
- E. Childhood
  - 1. Training
  - 2. Ceremonies
- F. Adult responsibilities
- G. Death rituals

IV. War and trade

    A. War

        1. Reasons for war

        2. Kinds of battles

    B. Trade

        1. Trading partners

        2. Trading items

V. Religion

    A. Ceremonies

        1. Dances and rhythn instruments

        2. Costumes

    B. Beliefs and myths

    C. Shamans

        1. Kinds of doctors

        2. Training of shamans

VI. Food

    A. Adults' jobs in food gathering

    B. Kinds of tribal foods, including army worms

    C. Food-gathering campsites

    D. Acorns

    E. Fishing methods

    F. Hunting methods

    G. Other uses of animal parts

VII. Tools, utensils, and weapons

    A. Plant uses

    B. Wood

    C. Stone

VIII. Baskets

    A. Kinds of weaving

    B. Types of baskets and uses

    C. Designs on baskets

IX. Clothing

    A. Men and children

    B. Women's clothing

    C. Cool weather clothing

    D. Ornaments and tattoos

X. History

    A. First meeting with white people

    B. Round Valley Reservation

    C. Tribal council formed in 1934

    D. Today's Yukis

        1. Land problems

        2. Importance of logging

        3. Today's population of Yuki tribal members

        4. Rachel Logan

GLOSSARY

AWL: a sharp, pointed tool used for making small holes in leather or wood

CEREMONY: a meeting of people to perform formal rituals for a special reason; like an awards ceremony to hand out trophies to those who earned honors

CHERT: rock which can be chipped off, or flaked, into pieces with sharp edges

COILED: a way of weaving baskets which looks like the basket is made of rope coils woven together

DIAMETER: the length of a straight line through the center of a circle

DOWN: soft, fluffy feathers

DROUGHT: a long period of time without water

DWELLING: a building where people live

FLETCHING: attaching feathers to the back end of an arrow to make the arrow travel in a straight line

GILL NET: a flat net hanging vertically in water to catch fish by their heads and gills

GRANARIES: basket-type storehouses for grains and nuts

HERITAGE: something passed down to people from their long-ago relatives

LEACHING: washing away a bitter taste by pouring water through foods like acorn meal

MORTAR: flat surface of wood or stone used for the grinding of grains or herbs with a pestle

PARCHING: to toast or shrivel with dry heat

PESTLE: a small stone club used to mash, pound, or grind in a mortar

PINOLE: flour made from ground corn

INDIAN RESERVATION: land set aside for Native Americans by the United States government

RITUAL: a ceremony that is always performed the same way

SEINE NET: a net which hangs vertically in the water, encircling and trapping fish when it is pulled together

SHAMAN: tribal religious men or women who use magic to cure illness and speak to spirit-gods

SINEW: stretchy animal tendons

STEATITE: a soft stone (soapstone) mined on Catalina Island by the Gabrielino tribe; used for cooking pots and bowls

TABOO: something a person is forbidden to do

TERRITORY: land owned by someone or by a group of people

TRADITION: the handing down of customs, rituals, and belief, by word of mouth or example, from generation to generation

TREE PITCH: a sticky substance found on evergreen tree bark

TWINING: a method of weaving baskets by twisting fibers, rather than coiling them around a support fiber

NATIVE AMERICAN WORDS
WE KNOW AND USE

PLANTS AND TREES
hickory
pecan
yucca
mesquite
saguaro

ANIMALS
caribou
chipmunk
cougar
jaguar
opossum
moose

STATES
Dakota – friend
Ohio – good river
Minnesota – waters that
   reflect the sky
Oregon – beautiful water
Nebraska – flat water
Arizona
Texas

FOODS
avocado
hominy
maize (corn)
persimmon
tapioca
succotash

GEOGRAPHY
bayou – marshy body of
   water
savannah – grassy plain
pasadena – valley

WEATHER
blizzard
Chinook (warm, dry wind)

FURNITURE
hammock

HOUSE
wigwam
wickiup
tepee
igloo

INVENTIONS
toboggan

BOATS
canoe
kayak

OTHER WORDS
caucus – group meeting
mugwump – loner politician
squaw – woman
papoose – baby

CLOTHING
moccasin
parka
mukluk – slipper
poncho

BIBLIOGRAPHY

Cressman, L. S. *Prehistory of the Far West.* Salt Lake City, Utah: University of Utah Press, 1977.

Geiger, Maynard, O.F.M., Ph.D. *The Indians of Mission Santa Barbara.* Santa Barbara, CA 93105: Franciscan Fathers, 1986.

Heizer, Robert F., volume editor. *Handbook of North American Indians; California, volume 8.* Washington, D.C.: Smithsonian Institute, 1978.

Heizer, Robert F. and Elsasser, Albert B. *The Natural World of the California Indians.* Berkeley and Los Angeles, CA; London, England: University of California Press, 1980.

Heizer, Robert F. and Whipple, M.A.. *The California Indians.* Berkeley and Los Angeles, CA; London, England: University of California Press, 1971.

Heuser, Iva. *California Indians.* PO Box 352, Camino, CA 95709: Sierra Media Systems, 1977.

Macfarlen, Allen and Paulette. *Handbook of American Indian Games.* 31 E. 2nd Street, Mineola, N.Y. 11501: Dover Publications, 1985.

Murphey, Edith Van Allen. *Indian Uses of Native Plants.* 603 W. Perkins Street, Ukiah, CA 95482: Mendocino County Historical Society, © renewal, 1987.

National Geographic Society. *The World of American Indians.* Washington, DC: National Geographic Society reprint, 1989.

Tunis, Edwin. *Indians.* 2231 West 110th Street, Cleveland, OH: The World Publishing Company, 1959.

Credits:
The Pollard Group, Inc., Tacoma, Washington 98409
Dona McAdam, Mac on the Hill, Seattle, Washington 98109

Acknowledgements:
Kim Walters, Library Director, and Richard Buchen,
Research Librarian, Braun Library, Southwest Museum

Special thanks
Many thanks to George Freeman, a Yuki-Wailaki man,
for his help in my research of the present-day Yuki tribe
and territory.